Preface

Thank you for all the support from everyone who has bought or read this book. I hope the knowledge will help you to become the Christian warrior that you really are.

This book is an introduction on how to enter the war into an unseen world and how to fight successfully into a victory that will change your life for the better.

I would like to tell you a little about myself and how God revealed to me how to fight for my life.

I am a Husband to a beautiful and strong god fearing wife. I also have 2 young boys who keep me on my toes constantly. Currently as I am writing this book I and my wife are expecting another child who will be my first daughter.

My first revelation with warfare prayer was unexpected. I heard the still voice in me say open your mouth and defend yourself at first I didn't understand what this meant. At the time when I heard the small voice I was going through it. My mind was so overwhelmed with worry and stress. I thought something bad was going to happen to me. I thought I was going to lose my job. All of this started to affect my life physical I had tension in my head I started having chest pains I even felt like I was going to pass out most mornings at work. I couldn't concentrate on anything my mind was just negative and hostile. There were times I didn't even want to come out of the house and no matter what anybody said to me I just could change my mind.

That day when I heard that still voice it was the worst I had ever felt my head started spinning my chest tightened up and my legs became weak I remember it like it was yesterday, the enemy was trying to take me out he was stealing all that I had with his lies and it was manifesting into my physical life. I just did not know what to do then I heard a still voice in the mist of

all the struggle it was crystal clear. It said my son open your mouth and defend yourself. At first I didn't understand what it meant then I heard it again open your mouth and pray instantly I felt a rage and I open my mouth and began to say you have no power over me NO! NO! you idiot leave me alone in Jesus name. As I said this instantly everything ceased I felt light and free. I phoned my wife straight away and told her everything. The first she said to me was you sound much better. The scripture that came to my head when she said that was from the abundance of the heart the mouth speaks.

So, this was my first encounter with warfare prayer.

Dedication

I would like to take this time to make a dedication to my wife and children for supporting me and helping get this book together. She heard me read it to her repeatedly where she probably knows it by heart.

Also, a big shout out to sevenpillars headship and family for encouraging me to put all my material together to write this book.

Attending sevenpillars ministry really challenged me to seek and find what god has put in me and to operate in the gifts and talents he has blessed me with.

I also learnt a lot about who I am and who's I am

Thank you sevenpillars you have really been a blessing in my life.

If you would like to be as blessed as I am to fellowship with sevenpillars

There website is

WWW.SEVENPILLARS.ORG.UK

Head pastors:

Pastor Calvin

Pastor Rani

CONTENTS

Prayer Warfare, Warfare Prayer

1. What is Prayer warfare

Prayer warfare is you fighting in the spiritual realm covered and backed up by the spirit of god. The physical realm we live in is a reflection of what is taking place in the spiritual realm.

When you are being overwhelmed in the physical realm with sickness, stress, financial issues and e.g. This could be a result of a spiritual attack.

When we are being attacked in the physical realm our natural instincts are to defend ourselves and the best form of defence is attack. So, our spiritual instincts should be the same. (ATTACK)

2. **How to use prayer warfare**

John chapter 6 verse 63

Jesus said the words I speak are spirit and life.

We fight in the spiritual realm with our words this is what prayer warfare is. The words we speak are also spirit and life

Proverbs chapter 18 verse 21

King Solomon in all his god given wisdom said the power of life and death is in the tongue. So, use your words to fight in the spirit to defend yourself. (ATTACK)

3. <u>What prayer warfare does</u>

Prayer warfare changes things. It is a type of prayer which strikes a mighty blow to your oppressor and their camp. It changes atmospheres and circumstances.

Prayer warfare reveals the solider you are in this unseen war. It builds up faith in you to fight in the unseen realm against the unseen enemy.

<u>Preparing for war</u>

Before you enter a war, you must be sure to have on the right equipment have the right tools and the right attitude, these vital attributes will help you on your journey to victory. The equipment we need is the full amour of god you must apply this to yourself before you start every battle.

The attitude you need to have, must be one without remorse. You must mean what you say and say what you mean. You cannot be in war and be standing still. Your mind (Attitude) your actions must line up with what you are saying.

When you are trying to enforce something with authority. You do not stand still and speak quietly. When you are enforcing you use your hands, you take steps and you shout.

Now you are ready to enter the war.

<u>Prayer</u>

I COME IN THE NAME OF JESUS CHRIST

I FASTEN THE BELT OF TRUTH WHICH IS MY
BELIEF IN THE GOSPEL OF JESUS CHRIST

I PUT ON THE BREASTPLATE OF
RIGHTEOUSNESS WHICH GUARDS MY HEART
AND VITAL ORGANS

I STRAP UP THE SHOES OF PEACE FOR MY FEET
TO WALK IN AND STAND ON THE GOSPEL OF
PEACE

I TAKE UP THE SHIELD OF FAITH TO EXTINGISH
ALL THE MISSILES AND FIERY DARTS OF SATAN
AND HIS ARMY

I PUT ON THE HELMET OF SALVATION TO GUARD MY MIND FROM ALL THE LIES OF THE OPPOSER

AND I HOLD TIGHT IN MY HAND THE SWORD OF THE SPIRIT WHICH IS THE UNCHANGEABLE WORD OF GOD TO STRIKE THE NECK OF ENEMY

I PLACE A HEDGE OF PROTECTION AROUND MYSELF AND ALL MY LOVED ONES, I COVER EVERY AREA OF MINE AND THEIR LIVES IN THE BLOOD OF JESUS

IN THE NAME OF JESUS

I NOW DECLARE WAR

LORD I STAND IN OBIDENCE TO YOUR WORD BELIEVING AND ACCEPTING IT AS THE TRUTH

(GIVE A LOUD SHOUT OF PRAISE)

LORD YOU SAID WHATEVER YOU BIND ON EARTH SHALL ME BOUND IN HEAVEN
I BIND HERE ON EARTH ALL THE STRONGMEN OF THE ENEMY COMING AGAINST

MY FAMILY   MY CHILDREN
        MY RELATIONSHIPS
MY MARRIAGE   MY HOME
        MY PROMISES
MY DREAMS   MY MONEY
        MY FAITH
MY BANK ACCOUNTS   MY HEALTH
        MY ASSETS
MY PEACE   MY JOY
        MY BLESSINGS
MY CALLING   MY PURPOSE
        MY CREATIVNESS
MY ANIONTING   MY ENTITLEMENT
        MY COURAGE
MY VISION   MY UNDERSTANDING
        MY HOPE
MY BELIEF   MY VICTORY
        MY PROSPERITY
MY AUTHORITY   MY OVERFLOW
        MY TIME
MY BREAKTHROUGH   MY HARVEST
        MY SEEDS
MY BODY   MY TONGUE
        MY MIRACLE
MY REVALATIONS   MY FRIENDS
        MY SLEEP
MY BUSINESS   MY JOB
        MY EMOTIONS

MY WILL	MY MIND
MY THOUGHTS	
MY REPUTATION	MY IDEAS
MY SALVATION	
MY FREEDOM	MY COMFORT
MY HEARING	
MY SIGHT	MY STRENGHT
MY HEART	
MY FUTURE	MY TESTIMONIES
MY HEALING	

THIS PRAYER IN THE NAME OF JESUS

I DISOWN AND RENOUNCE EVERY CURSE I HAVE RECEIVED ON PURPOSE OR BY ACCIDENT

BY THE POWER INVESTED IN ME THROUGH CHRIST JESUS I ANNILULATE DESTROY AND DISMANTLE ALL OBSTACLES AND ALL ALIEN OBJECTS ON MY PATH

I REJECT THE ENSNAREMENT OF THE ENEMY AGAINST MY MIND AND EMOTIONS

I SEVER THE NECK OF UNBELIEF, WORRY, FEAR, DOUBT, CONDEMNATION AND DEPRESSION

I CAST DOWN WITH FORCE IMAGINATIONS, THOUGHTS AND EVERY HIGH THING THAT EXALTS ITSELF TO THE KNOWLEDGE OF GOD

ALL SPIRITUAL ITES I COME AGAINST YOU WITH THE BLOOD OF JESUS

PERIZZITES, CANNAITES, HITTIES, AMORITES, GIRGASHITES, HIVITES AND JEBUSITES

LORD GIVE THEM ALL INTO MY HANDS TODAY

IN THE NAME OF JESUS

I DECLARE THAT ALL SPIRITUAL ITES HAVE BEEN DEMOLISHED, DESTROYED AND SCATTERED

IN THE NAME OF JESUS

ALL KINDS OF LACK AND STRUGGLE

EMOTIONAL, SPIRITUAL, FINANCIAL, PHYSICAL AND MENTAL

ARE TOTALLY AND UTTERLY CUT OF FROM MY EXISTENCE

I BURN ALL BRIDGES THAT JOIN YOU TO ME, EVERY UNDERPASS, EVERY ROPE OR ANYTHING THAT GIVES YOU ACCESS TO ME I DESTROY AND DEMOLISH

IN THE NAME JESUS

IN ME, ALL TRESURES THAT HAVE BEEN BURIED DEEP DUE TO CIRCUMSTANCES OR THINGS I HAVE BEEN THROUGH. I DIG YOU UP AND DECREE YOU ARE RELEASED

ALL IMPRISONMENT OF MY DREAMS, IDEAS AND MY VISIONS I COMMAND YOU TO RELEASE THEM NOW

IN THE NAME OF JESUS

SATAN I AM NOT ASKING BUT IM DEMANDING YOU TO GIVE BACK WITH INTREST WHAT EVER YOU HAVE STOLEN

I TAKE BACK BY FORCE VIOLENTLY ALL THAT I AM ENTITLED TO

IN THE NAME OF JESUS

I PULL AND TEAR DOWN ALL WALLS AND STRONG TOWERS, STANDING UP AGAINST OR SURROUNDING MY GOD GIVEN RIGHTS.

IN THE NAME OF JESUS

LORD YOU SAID WHATEVER YOU LOOSE ON EARTH SHALL BE LOOSE IN HEAVEN.

IN THE NAME OF JESUS

I LOOSE HERE ON EARTH ALL THE THINGS THAT BELONG TO ME! I COMMAND ALL THE STRONGMEN OF THE ENEMY TO LOOSE....

MY HEALING	MY HAVRVEST
MY ANSWERS	MY BREAKTHROUGH
MY FINANCES	MY MIRACLES
MY GOOD HEATLH	MY REVALATIONS
MY JOY	MY JOBS
MY PROMISES	MY FREEDOM
MY DREAMS	MY COMFORT
MY RELATIONSHIPS	MY HEARING
MY ASSETS	MY KINGSHIP
MY FAMILY	MY FRIENDS
MY BLESSINGS	MY GRAIN
MY IDEAS	MY OPPORTUNITIES
MY BUSINESS	MY WINE
MY VICTORYS	MY PEACE
MY AUTHORITY	MY RAIN

.

I NOW POSSESS THESE THINGS BY FAITH IN JESUS NAME.

(DECLARATIONS SAY WITH AUTHORITY)

I DECREE I SHALL INHABIT ALL THE PROMISES
OF GOD.
I DECLARE VICTORY IN EVERY AREA OF MY LIFE.
I DECREE I POSSES RESSURECTION POWER

I DECLARE THE WEALTH OF THE WICKED IS NO
LONGER STORED UP BUT HAS NOW BEEN
RELEASED UNTO ME THE RIGHTEOUS.

I DECLARE TOTAL HEALING

IN MY MIND
IN MY RELATIONSHIPS
IN MY FINANCES
IN MY HOME
IN MY BODY

I DECREE MY TONGUE SPEAKS LIFE.
I DECLARE MY TONGUE SHALL BE FOR
CONSTRUCTION AND NOT DEMOLITION.
I DECREE THAT OUT OF MY MOUTH SHALL
PROCEED BLESSINGS AND NOT CURSES.

I DECLARE I AM A KING

I AM APRIEST

I AM AN AMBASSADOR

IN JESUS NAME

I DECREE I AM ON TOP AND NOT BELOW
I DECLARE I AM THE HEAD AND NOT THE TAIL
I DECREE I AM A LENDER AND NOT A
BORROWER

I AM A SON NO LONGER A SLAVE
I AM FRIEND NO LONGER A SERVANT
I AM A BELIEVER NO LONGER A GENTILE

I AM BLAMELESS
I AM HOLY
I AM RIGHTEOUS
IN CHRIST JESUS

IN THE NAME OF JESUS

THANK YOU, LORD, FOR THE VICTORY

You have now taken authority you have woken
the Christian warrior within you. Get ready to
receive back whatever has been lost, stolen or
whatever you have been deprived of.
Pray this prayer daily with a great zeal believing
what you are saying and be expecting results.

MORNING PRAYER

THIS IS THE DAY THAT THE LORD HAS
MADE. I WILL REJOICE AND BE GLAD IN IT

LORD I THANK YOU FOR WAKING ME
THIS MORNING

I THANK YOU FOR ANOTHER DAY OF MY
LIFE

I THANK YOU FOR ANOTHER DAY OF
BLESSINGS AND VICTORIES

FATHER ORDER MY STEPS TODAY

IN THE NAME OF JESUS

**(ALWAYS APPLY YOUR FULL ARMOUR
FOR THE DAY AHEAD)**

I PUT ON THE BREASTPLATE OF
RIGHTEOUSNESS WHICH GUARDS MY
HEART AND VITAL ORGANS

I STRAP UP MY SHOES FOR MY FEET TO
WALK IN AND STAND ON THE GOSPEL OF
PEACE

I TAKE UP MY SHIELD OF FAITHTO
EXTINGUISH ALL FIERY DARTS OF SATAN
AND HIS ARMY

I PUT ON THE HELMET OF SALVATION TO
GUARD MY MIND FROM ALL THE LIES OF
THE ACCUSER

AND I HOLD IN MY HAND THE SWORD OF
THE SPIRIT WHICH IS THE
INDESTRUCTABLE WORD

LORD PLACE A HEDGE OF PROTECTION AROUND MYSELF, MY SPOUSE, MY CHILDREN, MY MARRIAGE, MY HOME, MY FINANCES, MY BUSINESS/JOB, MY MINISTRY AND ALL THAT GOD HAS GIVEN OR HAS GOT FOR ME

IN THE NAME OF JESUS

I COMMAND THIS DAY TO BE PRODUCTIVE AND PROSPEROUS

IN THIS DAY BLESSINGS SHALL TRACK ME DOWN AND I SHALL RECEIVE THEM ALL WITH RECEPTIVE ARMS AND HOLD FAST TO THEM

THANK YOU AGAIN LORD FOR ALL YOU HAVE DONE, ALL YOU ARE DOING AND ALL YOU ARE GOING TO DO

BLESS YOU MY BEAUTIFUL FATHER

SALVATION PRAYER

IF YOU HAVEN`T ALREADY AND WOULD LIKE TO BE BORN AGAIN. JUST SAY THIS SIMPLE PRAYER AND YOU WILL BE BORN AGAIN

HEAVENLY FATHER I REALIZE THAT I AM A SINNER AND I HAVE SINNED AGAINST YOU. I ASK YOU TO FORGIVE ME. I BELIEVE THAT YOUR SON JESUS DIED FOR ME, WAS RESSURECTED AND IS ALIVE TODAY.

JESUS COME INTO MY HEART, I CONFESS YOU AS MY LORD AND SAVIOUR

JESUS, THANK YOU FOR SAVING ME

IF YOU HAVE SAID THIS PRAYER, BY FAITH YOU ARE SAVED.

PRAYER

PRAYER

PRAYER

NOTES

NOTES

NOTES

NOTES

Printed in Great Britain
by Amazon